Part 1

Financial Shift

Destiny S. Harris

...

...

Copyright

Copyright © 2024 Destiny S. Harris.

All rights reserved. No part of this publication may be reproduced without prior written permission from the author, except in the case of quotations.

Book design by Destiny S. Harris.

First printing edition 2024.

www.destinyh.com

...

...

A Gift For You

Thank you for taking the time to read this book. As a token of my appreciation, here is a gift to you.

I give away free books daily. Here's how to get your free books today:

Step 1: Visit amazon.com/author/destinyharris

Step 2: Filter books by "Price: Low to High"

Step 3: Download available free eBooks

...

...

Table of Contents

Copyright 4

A Gift For You 7

Quick Bit 13

Introduction 16

Chapter 1: Golden Rules 23

Chapter 2: What Are Your Goals? 33

Thank You For Reading 36

The End. 39

About Destiny S. Harris 42

Connect W/ Destiny S. Harris 47

Free Gifts! 50

Please Leave A Review 52

Tell Me What You Want 54

...

...

Quick Bit

Thank you for taking the time to read this book.

My hope is that you leave at least 1% better than before you read this book and walk away with at least one takeaway.

I'd like to graciously ask that you help me by leaving a <u>review</u> of this book; your feedback helps me write better books and helps others get a glimpse of the book.

With Kindness,
Destiny

...

...

Introduction

The average American citizen has less than $500 in their savings account and has an average of $103,000 in debt (student loans, car loans, personal loans, mortgage loans, credit card debt, etc.), which means they're one situation away from being broke or they already are broke.

You were likely not taught about personal finance in school, and your family likely didn't educate you about the subject at home, so where does that leave you?

You likely suck (or aren't the best) at managing your money, budgeting, investing, planning for retirement, and living below your means.

Most people don't know how to manage their money because they follow what everyone else does.

They're managing their money by the default habits everyone else seems to adopt and implement:

1. Live above your means
2. Invest later
3. Participate in lifestyle creep
4. Don't actively learn about personal finance
5. Don't talk about money (it's rude)
6. Buy without intention

My parents started educating me about finance from a young age. As a young kid, I had a piggy bank and a bank account, and we read personal finance books at the dinner table. Then, they brought a financial advisor to our home to set me up with a ROTH IRA. All of this is rare. Most parents don't do this. I'm incredibly grateful my parents set me up for financial success, but I understand this is likely not your story.

Your parents likely didn't set you up, complained about money frequently, and manage debt to this day (or even need your financial help).

Though you likely didn't have the best financial upbringing, financial struggle doesn't have to be your financial destiny.

If you are tired of struggling financially, historically suck at money, consistently complain about prices, and always have an excuse for why you can't afford something, this book is for you.

As a kid, I knew I never wanted to struggle for money, as I had seen many people around me experience this.

You must arrive at a point where you're unwilling to settle for financial struggle, and the choice is always entirely up to you.

Do you want to thrive financially, or do you want to struggle financially?

To thrive financially, you must change what you're doing today.

You need to change what you're doing to change things in your life.

It sounds simple, but people often think that wishing, dreaming, and not doing much of anything different will get them results.

Incorrect.

You must shift our ways.

Once you change what you're doing, the magic appears, and you will start experiencing positive results in your financial affairs.

There is too much wealth in this universe to struggle financially, live paycheck to paycheck, and not be able to experience and live the way you desire.

Get off the bullsh*t and get your money right.

This book is going to be short, sweet, and straightforward. Each part of the series will only have three chapters.

I'm not here to keep you long, and I'm not here to confuse you. Let's get straight to the point so you can do better with your money.

If you don't understand something, be proactive and do a quick Google search.

...

Chapter 1: Golden Rules

There are a few golden rules you should always live by financially:

1. **Live below your means**

Never spend more than you earn.

2. **Invest (unlike the rest)**

Invest at least 10% or more of your income, and don't touch it. Leave it alone.

The longer you leave your money alone, the larger it grows due to compound interest.

Most people don't invest, so many end up in their retirement years without much money in their bank account.

Start investing now, and if you're close to your retirement years, start investing today. It's never too late.

3. **Avoid lifestyle inflation**

It's easy to increase your expenses as your income increases.

What's not easy is decreasing your expenses or keeping them the same as your income increases.

You don't have anything to prove to anyone, so don't go buying dumb shit that you don't need because everyone else is doing it or encouraging you to.

So many **broke** people have told me to go out and buy a new car to replace my almost two-decade-old car. I didn't listen to them. They're still broke, and I'm increasing my wealth.

You don't **have** to wear and use name-brand clothes, shoes, bags, and accessories.

You don't **have** to upgrade your phone and tech gadgets every year.

You don't **have** to live in the priciest home.

You don't **have** to spend your money as most people do.

You can use your money intentionally and focus on purchasing the items that bring you the most convenience and joy.

For example, I like to spend on food and travel. Those are my primary categories. What are yours?

4. **Multiple income sources**

Continuously diversify your income, so if you lose one income stream, another one still brings the moola in.

Make yourself economically bullet-proof by having multiple income streams **and** implementing number 5 below.

5. **Maintain an emergency fund.**

Shit happens. Maintain an emergency fund instead of worrying about what may or may not happen.

It doesn't mean something terrible is going to happen.

Usually, nothing terrible happens; inconveniences happen (e.g., your car needs repairs).

Avoid going into debt over inconveniences by maintaining an emergency fund.

Your emergency fund should, at minimum, hold at least three months' worth of expenses. If your monthly expenses equate to $3,000, your bare minimum emergency fund should total $9,000.

Now, I'm going to stretch you. Ideally, I encourage you to have 12 months of emergency expenses. You can keep this money in multiple accounts that are not easily accessible.

The goal is to only pull this money out for emergencies. A wedding, a last-minute vacation, eating out, and a night out on the town do **NOT** qualify as emergencies.

Sorry chip.

6. Self-Educate Relentlessly

My parents had my siblings, and I read personal finance books at the dinner table. The only difference between me and others who have the opportunity to learn about finance at a young age is that I never stopped reading personal finance books. I kept reading them and still read them to this day. There is so much information about personal finance that I don't know, and the learning journey will never end. Stay hungry for knowledge so you can better your financial outcomes.

If you continually educate yourself about money, you will inevitably make more intelligent decisions with your money. It's impossible to fail when you have the proper knowledge at your fingertips.

Don't know how to invest? Read a book, listen to a podcast, attend a free seminar, do some research, and learn for yourself.

Not knowing how or understanding what to do with your money is not a legitimate excuse to fail and suck at the personal finance game.

If you suck at money, that's on you. It's not on your parents. It's not on the school system. It's not on the government. It's on you.

If you can watch videos on social media, you can watch videos about personal finance.

If you can watch television, you can watch a documentary about money.

. . .

...

Chapter 2: What Are Your Goals?

What are your financial goals? More specifically:

1. What are your retirement goals?

2. How much do you want to have in your emergency fund?

3. How much money do you desire to earn annually?

4. How much money do you want to maintain in your bank account?

5. How much debt do you have, and when do you want to pay off all your debts?

6. How much money do you want to spend each month?

7. How many income streams do you want to build and maintain?

8. When do you want to retire?

9. What does financial freedom look and feel like for you?

10. What are some things you want to buy?

11. What generous/community efforts would you like to get involved with to help others?

12. What personal finance subjects do you want to explore to develop a deeper understanding?

Without goals, you will drift. Most people suck at money because they don't have any knowledge, **nor** do they have any financial goals.

Just wanting to do better and having enough money is not good enough; it's too vague.

Paint a clear picture of your needs, wants, and motivations, then dive into defining the steps to reach those goals.

13. The final question: What limiting thoughts and beliefs do you have about money that could limit your financial goals and progress?

You likely have adopted beliefs about money from parents, friends, and society. It's essential to identify which ones could be sabotaging your financial progress.

Thank You For Reading

Thank you for reading this book.

Stay loved, blessed, lucky, favored, aware, joyous, enlightened, and committed to bettering yourself.

...

...

The End.

...

...

About Destiny S. Harris

Destiny S. Harris' goal is to positively inspire, cultivate, elevate, and educate the minds of individuals across the globe through her writing.

Creating (whether books, courses, articles, poetry, or music) has always been Destiny's thing, not to mention health & fitness and all things entrepreneurial.

Destiny published her first book, "Beauty Secrets for Girls," at age 11 and her second book, "Don't Wait Until It's Too Late," at age 12.

Destiny obtained three degrees in Psychology, Political Science, & Women's Studies. She also started her own music teaching business at the age of 14, which she led for over ten years. In addition, she has been teaching academic, career, and personal development topics to thousands of students and readers since 2004.

Outside of writing, Destiny loves and enjoys many activities: reading, weightlifting, walking, biking, traveling, football (and sports in general), dogs, animals, food, classic movies, quality and new experiences, mountain and ocean views, sleeping, plants, and nature.

Check out her work, leave a review, share your thoughts with your friends and family, and participate in a movement: **Serving others through self-education (books).**

Complete the Steps To Get Free eBooks:

Step 1: Go to amazon.com/author/destinyharris

Step 2: Filter books by "Price: Low to High"

Step 3: Download available free books

...

...

Connect W/ Destiny S. Harris

Please reach out and stay in touch. Start a conversation today @ destinyh.com

...

...

Free Gifts!

Access courses & free eBooks at the link below:

destinyh.com

. . .

Please Leave A Review

If this book impacts you in some way, please let me know by dropping a review on it.

I write better books with **your** input.

...

Tell Me What You Want

I've written many books, but if you don't see what you're looking for or need, get in touch with me via my website, articles, comments, or reviews, and let me know what you're looking for so I can create it for you. I'm here to serve.

Destiny

...

...

www.ingramcontent.com/pod-product-compliance
Lightning Source LLC
Chambersburg PA
CBHW030052230526
45471CB00003B/1058